Instant Migration to HTML5 and CSS3 How-to

Discover how to upgrade your existing website to the latest HTML5 and CSS3 standards

Dushyant Kanungo

[PACKT] PUBLISHING

BIRMINGHAM - MUMBAI

Instant Migration to HTML5 and CSS3 How-to

First published: January 2013

Production Reference: 1160113

Published by Packt Publishing Ltd.
Livery Place
35 Livery Street
Birmingham B3 2PB, UK.

ISBN 978-1-84969-574-9

`www.packtpub.com`

Credits

Author
Dushyant Kanungo

Reviewer
Daniel Buzzo

Acquisition Editor
Erol Staveley

Commissioning Editor
Ameya Sawant

Technical Editor
Dennis John

Copy Editor
Alfida Paiva

Project Coordinator
Esha Thakker

Proofreader
Maria Gould

Graphics
Melwyn D'sa

Production Coordinator
Melwyn D'sa

Cover Work
Melwyn D'sa

Cover Image
Aditi Gajjar

About the Author

Dushyant Kanungo has more than 10 years of professional experience in web design and development. A graduate of Web Design from the University of the West of England, Bristol, his core interests are information architecture, human-computer interaction, and the principles of web design.

In the past, he has served many world-renowned clients such as Sony Ericsson, Dyson Ltd., Hilton Hotels, and Bausch & Lomb, among others.

Dushyant is a native of Indore, India and currently lives in Bristol, United Kingdom.

You can visit Dushyant at `http://www.dushyantkanungo.com` or follow him on Twitter `(Twitter handle @dushyantmk)`.

I'd like to thank Mr. Daniel Buzzo for being an amazing teacher and guide and for taking pains to technically review this book. Also, thanks to Ameya and Esha from PACKT Publishing for being helpful and supporting in the process.

In the end, I'd like to thank my wife Priyanka, my brother Abhishek, and my sister Aarti for consistently bugging me about the progress and my pace of writing this book.

About the Reviewer

Daniel Buzzo is an artist, designer, researcher, and an educator working with new media and creative technologies. His primary interests are in media art, web platforms, interaction design, and digital media. With a career in interactive media spanning 25 years, he has been designing for the World Wide Web from its earliest beginnings.

He is a program leader for Digital Media at the University of the West of England, an established independent media artist, and a lead designer and co-owner at Buzzodesign, a UK based creative consultancy.

An alumnus of the Royal College of Art, his work has been shown internationally and appeared in publications as diverse as The Face, The Guardian, and Revolver. Alongside this, he has created interactive media for clients, including BBC TV, Volkswagen, and Reuters, and has also been involved in creating music projects for artists such as Talking Heads, The Orb, and Nine Inch Nails.

www.PacktPub.com

Support files, eBooks, discount offers and more

You might want to visit www.PacktPub.com for support files and downloads related to your book.

Did you know that Packt offers eBook versions of every book published, with PDF and ePub files available? You can upgrade to the eBook version at www.PacktPub.com and as a print book customer, you are entitled to a discount on the eBook copy. Get in touch with us at service@packtpub.com for more details.

At www.PacktPub.com, you can also read a collection of free technical articles, sign up for a range of free newsletters and receive exclusive discounts and offers on Packt books and eBooks.

PACKTLIB®

http://PacktLib.PacktPub.com

Do you need instant solutions to your IT questions? PacktLib is Packt's online digital book library. Here, you can access, read, and search across Packt's entire library of books.

Why Subscribe?

- Fully searchable across every book published by Packt
- Copy and paste, print and bookmark content
- On demand and accessible via web browser

Free Access for Packt account holders

If you have an account with Packt at www.PacktPub.com, you can use this to access PacktLib today and view nine entirely free books. Simply use your login credentials for immediate access.

To my father, Mr. Mahesh Kanungo.

Table of Contents

Preface 1

Instant Migration to HTML5 and CSS3 How-to 5

- Analysis of the current website (Must know) 6
- The migration begins (Must know) 11
- Microformats – the smarter Web (Should know) 21
- Play it on – multimedia (Must know) 26
- The mobile – the seamless experience (Become an expert) 29
- RIA – Canvas (Become an expert) 33
- CSS3 – beautiful yet powerful (Should know) 38
- Data – smart websites (Become an expert) 44
- The transferrable Web (Must know) 49

Preface

Adoption of a new technology is always a challenging process, especially when it poses as an improvement of a popular and well recognized benchmark technology. The delay and doubts over HTML5 and CSS3 is the best-case example in this scenario. Doubts about browser compatibility and resources required to upgrade websites keep most companies, developers, and managers from making the switch.

Moreover, the new HTML5 specifications were announced by the World Wide Web Consortium in 2010, and some parts of the specifications are still under consideration by its working committee.

Instant Migration to HTML5 and CSS3 How-to tries to attend to those trivial queries of the web development community in general. This book guides developers or designers with examples from everyday code to help them with quick migration to the latest web standard.

The book is also useful for students who are new to web development or design to get a grip over the latest HTML5 elements and CSS3 properties.

Not only have we tried to keep the book within the reach of most common browser-compatible development practices, we have also included alternative solutions for better websites.

What this book covers

Analysis of the current website (Must know): Before the migration of a website, we need to analyze and check the current website to get an outline list of all the features and tags that can be upgraded or must be made available for too-old browsers.

The migration begins (Must know): In this recipe, we will take an existing webpage and convert it into HTML5 without disturbing any of the previous content or structure of the website. We will start with the document declaration and end with the most common structural elements of the website.

Microformats – the smarter Web (Should know): This recipe will discuss microformats and their everyday application in hCards and author-based content. Though microformats existed before the specifications of HTML5, their importance in structural data is now higher than ever.

Play it on – multimedia (Must know): Here, we will talk about the native file formats for video and audio, which are integral parts of the new specifications. This allows the web pages to be independent from third-party plugins.

The mobile – the seamless experience (Become an expert): This recipe will discuss how the websites with HTML5 can be rendered with the same efficiency on various devices, including tablet PCs and mobile phones, with the use of media queries. We will also discuss the advantages of WebKit-based browsers and support techniques.

RIA – Canvas (Become an expert): This recipe will give a brief introduction of the interactive Rich Internet Application platform with HTML5 and CSS3. We will discuss a few basic possible applications of Canvas in routine websites.

CSS3 – beautiful yet powerful (Should know): This recipe will give a brief introduction of CSS3. We will discuss how you can use CSS3 to optimize and push its limits in HTML5.

Data – smart websites (Become an expert): This recipe will discuss HTML5's new DOM manipulation techniques for web messaging sockets and local storage.

The transferrable Web (Must know): In this recipe we will review the web page that we started migrating in the beginning and will compare it with the initial code.

What you need for this book

This book is written keeping in mind existing developers and designers who have previous knowledge of HTML and CSS.

Who this book is for

The book will help anyone who is willing to upgrade their skill set and wishes to migrate from XHTML or HTML to HTML5.

Students who have learned HTML on a beginner level can directly jump to HTML5's latest elements and CSS3 properties, without worrying about having full-fledged knowledge of previous W3C specifications.

Reader feedback

Feedback from our readers is always welcome. Let us know what you think about this book—what you liked or may have disliked. Reader feedback is important for us to develop titles that you really get the most out of.

To send us general feedback, simply send an e-mail to feedback@packtpub.com, and mention the book title via the subject of your message.

If there is a book that you need and would like to see us publish, please send us a note in the **SUGGEST A TITLE** form on www.packtpub.com or e-mail suggest@packtpub.com.

If there is a topic that you have expertise in and you are interested in either writing or contributing to a book, see our author guide on www.packtpub.com/authors.

Customer support

Now that you are the proud owner of a Packt book, we have a number of things to help you to get the most from your purchase.

Downloading the example code

You can download the example code files for all Packt books you have purchased from your account at http://www.PacktPub.com. If you purchased this book elsewhere, you can visit http://www.PacktPub.com/support and register to have the files e-mailed directly to you.

Errata

Although we have taken every care to ensure the accuracy of our content, mistakes do happen. If you find a mistake in one of our books—maybe a mistake in the text or the code—we would be grateful if you would report this to us. By doing so, you can save other readers from frustration and help us improve subsequent versions of this book. If you find any errata, please report them by visiting http://www.packtpub.com/support, selecting your book, clicking on the **errata submission form** link, and entering the details of your errata. Once your errata are verified, your submission will be accepted and the errata will be uploaded on our website, or added to any list of existing errata, under the Errata section of that title. Any existing errata can be viewed by selecting your title from http://www.packtpub.com/support.

Piracy

Piracy of copyright material on the Internet is an ongoing problem across all media. At Packt, we take the protection of our copyright and licenses very seriously. If you come across any illegal copies of our works, in any form, on the Internet, please provide us with the location address or website name immediately so that we can pursue a remedy.

Please contact us at copyright@packtpub.com with a link to the suspected pirated material.

We appreciate your help in protecting our authors, and our ability to bring you valuable content.

Questions

You can contact us at `questions@packtpub.com` if you are having a problem with any aspect of the book, and we will do our best to address it.

Instant Migration to HTML5 and CSS3 How-to

Since its inception in 1991, HTML has changed only a handful of times. In this fast-paced digital age, it is very unusual for one of the most popular technologies to change so slowly. From the table-based layouts to div-based architectures, from HTML's primary specifications to backward-compatible XHTML websites, from inline styling to external dynamic stylesheets, the adoption of the technological advancement has progressed at a snail's pace.

Right after December 1999, when the HTML 4.01 specification was published, the focus of the **World Wide Web Consortium** (**W3C**) and the working groups shifted to XHTML and CSS. The move of jumping between various coding practices, for simple tag-based documentation and for fallback compatibilities to earlier versions, has left a majority of the web pages with broken, inconsistent, and nonstandard-oriented code.

In today's times, when a web presence is considered equal to a real estate or shop front, it becomes essential for the web pages to be accessible, efficient, lean, fast, and semantically correct for higher visibility in the search results.

Welcome to the *Instant Migration to HTML5 and CSS3 How-to* handbook. This book will provide you with all the information that you need to get up to speed while migrating your current website to HTML5, the new web standard by W3C.

In the coming recipes, we will go through various examples to help you migrate your current website without changing any of the existing content/presentation to HTML5. We will also address any compatibility issues that your website might face in the process and suggest appropriate solutions, and further discuss some excellent new features of the upgrade.

Analysis of the current website (Must know)

Before the migration of any website, we need to analyze and check the current state of documents and visitors. This exercise will help us in getting an outline of all the resources, libraries, and dependencies that can be upgraded.

A quick analysis of visitors will help us determine the most common browsers used by visitors and whether there is any specific browser (read IE6) that we can exclude from this upgrade. If a large part of the visitors' demographic is consistently using outdated browsers to access your website, this gathered information will guide us in setting the code rules or fallback options for those visitors.

Getting ready

To begin the analysis, all we need is access to Google Analytics, or a similar tracking service integrated in the website's dashboard. For example, we will have a look at the visitor trends of my website, which is `http://www.dushyantkanungo.com`, for a certain duration of time.

You can do it with your current website and a word processor (pencil/paper) to keep track of issues we find on our way.

How to do it...

1. The website `http://www.dushyantkanungo.com` uses Google Analytics for visitor tracking, which can be accessed from `http://www.google.com/analytics`. After navigating to **Audience** | **Technology** | **Browser & OS** from the left-hand side column, here is what we get for a specific period:

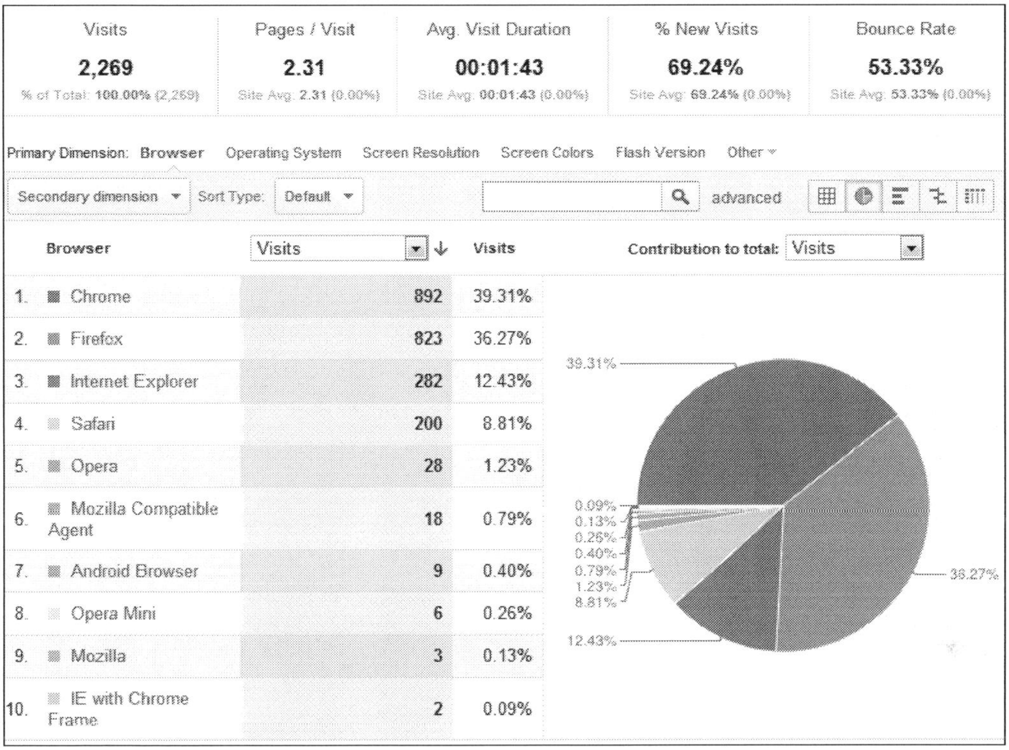

Based on the preceding stats provided by Google Analytics, we now know that over 75 percent of the visitors to this website were using either Google Chrome or Firefox and about 20 percent traffic was generated from IE and Safari.

2. Moving further in, we can see that the ratio of the older versions of IE, which were used to visit the website, becomes nominal and hence, we can choose coding practices to either support or exclude them.

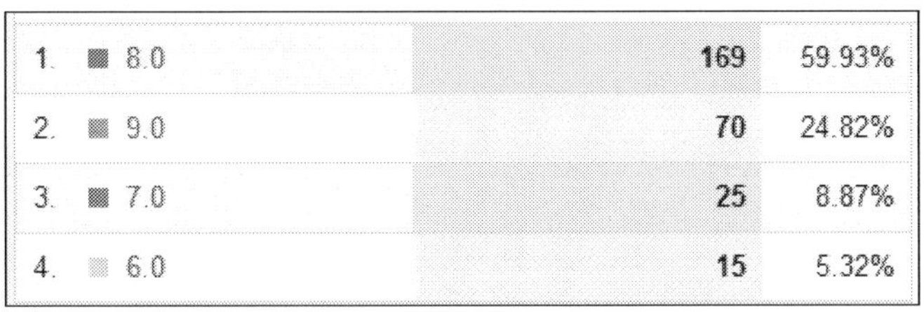

1.	8.0	169	59.93%
2.	9.0	70	24.82%
3.	7.0	25	8.87%
4.	6.0	15	5.32%

A similar analysis with operating systems can tell us about the number of visitors coming from mobile devices or varying screen resolutions. This helps us in designing the support for a range of end users in the target demographic.

3. Next, we need to check the current validation status of the website with a W3C validator at `http://validator.w3.org`. This will tell us if there are any known issues with the content markup before we head towards the updated version. Just note down or copy the errors in a document for future reference.

> Sometimes, old websites have links to external resources that may have moved or no longer exist. Broken links from a web page are always frowned upon, not just by the visitors but also by the crawlers as well.
>
> To examine the current status of those links and to rectify them in due course, we can use a small utility called **Xenu's Link Sleuth** (download it from `http://xenus-link-sleuth.en.softonic.com`), which is a portable freeware, to generate a report on any broken link the site may have.

4. Moving ahead, using Firefox or Chrome, you can check the time taken by the page to load by right-clicking anywhere on the page and selecting **Inspect Element** | **Network**. Then we have to refresh the page to see the real-time results of the time taken by all the requests to the server from the page.

5. You may like to check whether scripts for external widgets or any large image file is taking a long time to load, hampering the performance of the website.

How it works...

The knowledge of the target audience, browsers, known content-based broken mark-up information, and linking structure will help you improve the final migrated product quality.

Also, you may wish to move from old DHTML/JavaScript utilities to improved jQuery libraries, or image-based text to CSS-driven styling for healthy performance.

There's more...

The relevance of HTML5 is far greater than one expects from a new set of rules to write web pages. The simple yet powerful tag comes with a lot of expectations from developers as well.

Impact of valid code

The **Document Type Definition** (**DTD**), represented as `<!DOCTYPE...>`, allows browsers to correctly interpret which rules (XHTML, HTML, and so on) have been used to write individual web pages, and subsequently render them correctly.

Generic specification for HTML, and later for XHTML, allows browsers to render the web page with the best solution possible with or without the valid use of HTML tags. This means, if a document is written with a defined DTD as XHTML, it will still render and display all the elements that are not closed with specifications of XHTML (for example `<br/>`).

The whole point of migrating to a higher standard lies in adopting the optimum practices to develop the code so that it can pave the way for future technological developments. The biggest argument from browser vendors for not supporting all the specifications from W3C on HTML or CSS, remains the lower popularity of the current standards and wide numbers of web pages still being developed with faulty coding practices.

As a web professional, it is important for us to make sure that we are developing web pages that are up to the international standards, semantically correct, and endorse the whole purpose of the Internet as a stateless, ownerless, and free network to keep the browser vendors on the edge of their seats.

Importance of HTML5

It is not that difficult to understand the reason behind so much hullabaloo and noise about HTML5. To put things in a clear perspective, here are 5 S's of HTML5:

- **File size**: The file size differences with HTML5 using new semantic sectioning tags will be marginally smaller than XHTML. With various new tags for tasks that needed external support or longer syntaxes, we have a much cleaner and more powerful HTML specification now.
- **Semantics**: The semantics of HTML5 standardizes existing coding practices to help machines and humans alike, in reading and understanding the code. This also paves the way for scalable and maintenance-friendly websites.
- **Simplicity**: New easy tags prove more than helpful in defining the structure of the document than ever before. This keeps the structure simple and easy to understand during maintenance or handover.
- **Support**: With wide varieties of devices and browser support, it is now easier to create rich web-based applications without depending on third-party plugins on the visitor end. Combined with CSS3, HTML5 comes up with everything from beautiful typography to external fonts, gradient colors to rounded edges, and much more.
- **SEO**: For business owners and marketing managers, HTML5 migration proves to be an asset investment, which has a strong potential of returns in the long run. With higher content-to-code ratio, semantically located articles, and previously available (and actively encouraged with HTML5) microformats data, it is far easier for search crawlers to differentiate between genuine information and forced SEO practices.

The Semantic Web in a nutshell

According to the W3C:

> *"The Semantic Web provides a common framework that allows data to be shared and reused across application, enterprise, and community boundaries."*

In simple terms, this means that distinct modules of a web page such as header, footer, content, and so on can be individually identified and extracted by specific applications and crawlers for various purposes. Semantics in HTML5 gives an identity to the one-dimensional `DIV` tags and helps the websites to be smarter and encourages genuine content-based web pages.

Here is an example of a very fundamental structural difference which we will discuss in detail later on:

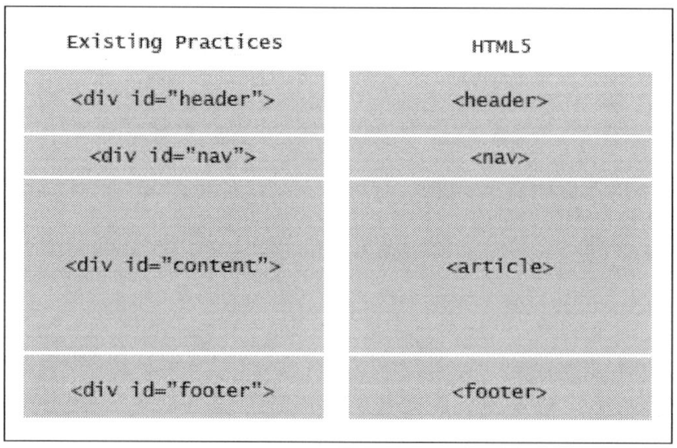

Presently, the developers can give IDs of their own choice to style any `DIV` tag within the web page. The `ID` for `DIV` of **content** can be `inner-copy` or the `ID` for `DIV` of **header** can be `top` and so on in the current practices with XHTML and HTML's older versions. This makes it impossible for external applications or crawlers to identify the actual content from spam data on the web page.

With HTML5, the new tags such as `HEADER`, `FOOTER`, `NAV`, `ARTICLE`, `ASIDE`, or `SECTION`, to name a few, provide a global identification system for various sections of a web page.

Finally

Armed with all the information necessary about the current website and with a clear purpose of the exercise, we begin the migration to HTML5.

We will also look at priority hacks and alternate solutions, which can solve some of these issues.

The migration begins (Must know)

In this section, we will take a sample XHTML page with routine features or sections, and will transform it into HTML5 without disturbing any of the previous content or structure of the website.

Getting ready

First off, get a local copy of your website from FTP and take a backup in some other folder for a comparison later. Open one of the HTML documents in the editor.

How to do it...

1. The example document's code may look something like the following code:

```
<!--the doctype declaration and head element-->
<!DOCTYPE html PUBLIC "-//W3C//DTD XHTML 1.0 Transitional//EN"
"http://www.w3.org/TR/xhtml1/DTD/xhtml1-transitional.dtd">
<html xmlns="http://www.w3.org/1999/xhtml" lang="en"
xml:lang="en">
<head>
<meta http-equiv="Content-Type" content="text/html;
charset="utf-8" />
<title>Example Document</title>
<link rel="stylesheet" type="text/css" href="style.css" />
</head>
<!--body of the document starts -->
<body>
<div id="wrapper">
<div id="header">
        <h1>HTML5 Migration</h1>
        <h2>A quick handbook for developers</h2>
</div>
<!--navigation starts-->
<div id="nav">
       <ul>
<li><a href="#">Home</a></li>
<li><a href="#">Chapters</a></li>
<li><a href="#">About</a></li>
   <li><a href="#">Contact</a></li>
</ul>
```

```
</div>
<!--navigation ends-->
<!--content starts-->
<div id="content">
        <h1>Article heading</h1>
        <h2>Article sub-heading</h2>
        <p>Loremipsumdolor sit amet, consecteturadipiscingelit.
Aeneanpharetraerosquis nisi pellentesque tempus
facilisisjustocommodo.</p>
        <p>Donecodioerat, euismod id posuere sit amet,
sollicitudin at nibh. Vivamuspharetra magna portaliberoiaculis
tempus.</p>
</div>
<!--sidebar starts-->
<div id="sidebar">
      <h2>Sidebar</h2>
<ul>
   <li>Item One</li>
   <li>Item Two</li>
   <li>Item Three</li>
   <li>Item Four</li>
   <li>Item Five</li>
   </ul>
</div>
<!--sidebar ends-->
<!--footer starts-->
<div id="footer">
        <p>&copy; 2012 PACKT Publishing &amp; Dushyant Kanungo.
All rights reserved.</p>
</div>
<!--footer ends-->
</div>
<!--content ends-->
</body>
<!--body ends--></html>
<!--end of document-->
```

2. Let's add a bit of styling to the preceding HTML page:

```
//style for the whole document
body {font-family: Verdana, Geneva, sans-serif;      font-size:
12px; color: #333; font-size:0.8em;}
//various div properties
div#wrapper {width:80%; margin: 0 auto;}
div#header, div#nav, div#footer {clear:both;}
div#header, div#nav, div#footer, div#content, div#sidebar
{margin:5px; border:1px solid #999; padding:10px;}
div#content {width:72%;float:left;}
div#sidebar {width:22%;float:left;}

div#nav ul {margin:0; padding:0;}
div#nav ul li {display:inline; margin-right:30px;}
div#footer {font-size:0.7em; color:#000;}
```

3. This is how the page looks in the browser:

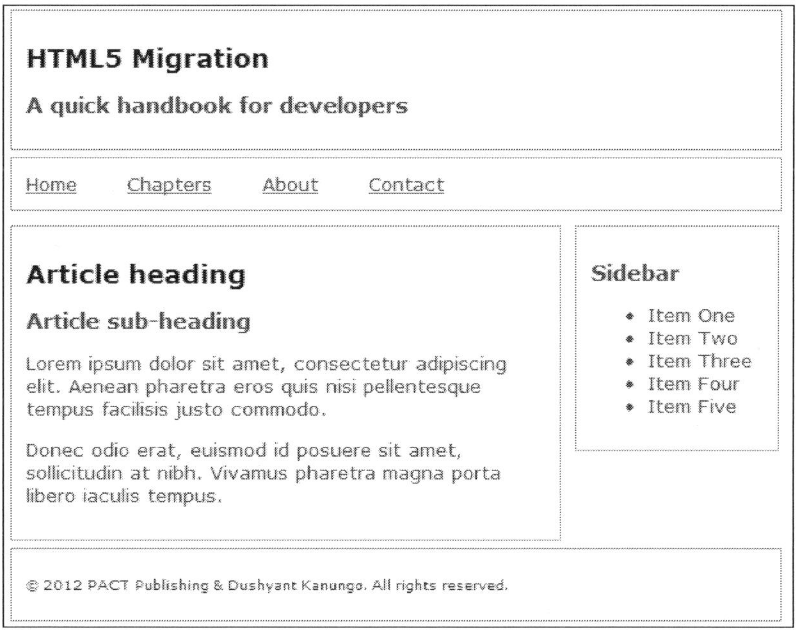

Downloading the example code

You can download the example code files for all Packt books you have purchased from your account at `http://www.PacktPub.com`. If you purchased this book elsewhere, you can visit `http://www.PacktPub.com/support` and register to have the files e-mailed directly to you.

The DOCTYPE

Browsers identify the documents' type, based on the Document Type Definition (DTD), which is declared in the first line of the preceding code by using the `DOCTYPE` tag. DTDs define specific rules for the markup language.

The DTD in the example code, which is in XHTML 1.0 with transitional rules, is defined as follows:

```
<!DOCTYPE html PUBLIC "-//W3C//DTD XHTML 1.0 Transitional//EN"
"http://www.w3.org/TR/xhtml1/DTD/xhtml1-transitional.dtd">
```

The `DOCTYPE` definition for HTML and XHTML documents varies between various versions and different rule sets such as `transitional`, `loose`, `strict`, or `frameset`. The problem of memorizing many different lines of code for various document versions or rule definitions is resolved in HTML5 by just using:

```
<!DOCTYPE HTML>
```

Short and simple.

The root element

Moving ahead, we come to the root element with the following code:

```
<html xmlns="http://www.w3.org/1999/xhtml" lang="en" xml:lang="en">
```

As we have already established the document type with `DOCTYPE` in the first line of the code, there is no need to declare it again. This truncates the tag to its primary form with the following language declaration:

```
<html lang="en">
```

The head element

The first thing that we declare in the head of any HTML page is for the character encoding. This makes the browser understand and helps translate if we have used any special character in the content. The character encoding is defined within a `Meta` tag:

```
<meta http-equiv="Content-Type" content='text/html; charset="utf-8"'>
```

And once again, this requires a declaration of content type for the third time in one page. After removing the unwanted code and repetitive declarations, this truncates to the following:

```
<meta charset="utf-8">
```

By looking at the migrated code up to this point, we get the following:

```
<!DOCTYPE html>
<html lang="en">
<head>
```

```
<meta charset="utf-8" />
<title>Example Document</title>
<link rel="stylesheet" type="text/css" href="style.css" />
</head>
```

The body element

The simplifies the `div` elements for common HTML documents as follows:

```
<div id="header">...</div>
<div id="nav">... </div>
<div id="content">... </div>
<div id="sidebar">... </div>
<div id="footer">... </div>
```

HTML5 gives us a universal identification for these `DIV` tags for individual identification:

```
<header>... </header>
<nav>... </nav>
<article>... </article>
<section>... </section>
<footer>... </section>
```

The `DIV` tag `sidebar` can be identified as unique with the `<aside>` tag.

Let us put all the new tags in the main code and here is what it will look like:

```
<div id="wrapper">
<header>
      <h1>HTML5 Migration</h1>
      <h2>A quick handbook for developers</h2>
</header>
<nav>
<ul>
<li><a href="#">Home</a>
</li>
</ul>
</nav>
<article>
      <h1>Article heading</h1>
      <h2>Article sub-heading</h2>
      <p>Loremipsumdolor … tempus. </p>
</article>
<aside>
   <h2>Sidebar</h2>
<ul>
<li>Item O... Five</li>
</ul>
</aside>
```

```
<footer>
        <p>&copy; 2012 PACKT … </p>
</footer>
</div>
```

Please note that HTML5 does not have any `<wrapper>` or `<container>` tags, and the use of the `DIV` tag is still a valid and acceptable practice with HTML5. The `<div id="wrapper">` or `<div id="container">` tag declarations are still commonly used to define the actual width of the page.

The CSS

With the newly truncated HTML code, we need to change the CSS as well. The CSS with HTML5 as elements helps in reducing CSS selectors for many tag elements. Hence, no prefixes are required for `CLASS` or `ID` designations on sectioning tags in the stylesheet for these elements; for example, `p.intro` and so on.

```
header, nav, footer {clear:both;}
header,nav,footer,article,aside {margin:5px; border:1px solid #999;
padding:10px;}
article {width:72%;float:left;}
aside {width:22%;float:left;}

nav ul {margin:0; padding:0;}
nav ul li {display:inline; margin-right:30px;}
footer {font-size:0.7em; color:#000;}
```

The compatibility scenarios

At present, only few, less popular browsers support all the block-based display for the new tags. To solve this problem, we have to create the definitions for browsers that *do not* yet understand the new semantic sectioning tags shown. Some browsers (certain versions of Internet Explorer) will need these to be explicitly created.

In order to define this, we just need to add the preceding code snippet at the top of the CSS file:

```
article,aside,details,figcaption,figure,footer,header,hgroup,menu,nav,
section {display:block;}
```

Further semantic sections

If you look closely at the code that we are using in the example, you will find that there are two `H1` and `H2` tags in constant use. One is for the header in the web page and another is for the content. This may result in confusion for the crawlers and may result in multiple occurrences of the headings on some pages.

To sort this issue, we can define *header groups* or the `HGROUP` element.

Here, the first set of headers become:

```
<header>
<hgroup>
         <h1>HTML5 Migration</h1>
      <h2>A quick handbook for developers</h2>
   </hgroup>
</header>
```

And the second group becomes:

```
<article>
   <hgroup>
         <h1>Article heading</h1>
         <h2>Article sub-heading</h2>
      </hgroup>
         <p>Loremipsumdolor … tempus. </p>
</article>
```

For multiple header occurrences on the page, which acts as a landing page for a particular section of articles, this can be appended for easy manipulation for a specific group:

```
<article>
   <hgroup>
         <h1>Article heading</h1>
         <h2>Article sub-heading</h2>
      </hgroup>
         <p>Loremipsumdolor … tempus. </p>

<hr>
   <hgroup>
         <h1>Article heading</h1>
         <h2>Article sub-heading</h2>
      </hgroup>
         <p>Loremipsumdolor … tempus. </p>
</article>
```

The styling for the headers can be done with the following selectors:

```
header hgroup {font-weight:bold;}
article hgroup {font-weight:normal;}
aside hgroup {text-decoration:none;}
```

This not only makes it easy to manipulate any specific set of headings, but also helps in generating a neat CSS file.

Figures and captions

If we look at all the textbooks or newspapers, it is a common practice to use figure captions with each image or graphic to provide a complete visual explanation. Looking at the web pages with the plain `<img>` element, we have to provide captions using a manual `div` element with all the additional properties associated with it.

```
<img src="images/sunset.jpg" alt="Sunset in Greece">
```

HTML5 allows us to chunk out figures and images with the `FIGURE` element and caption with a nested `FIGCAPTION` element:

```
<figure>
<img src="images/sunset.jpg" alt="Sunset in Greece">
<figcaption>A beautiful sunset in Greece by
<a href="http://www.flickr.com/photos/byrdiegyrl/"> Karol M</a>
</figcaption>
</figure>
```

This will output the following:

A beautiful sunset in Greece by Karol M

Use a small styling for the center alignment of the caption, if needed, and we have a semantically correct graphic, which also by abides the accessibility and **Creative Commons** rules.

Form elements

Form elements in the previous versions of HTML were highly dependent on JavaScript support for certain basic tasks such as **placeholders** and **required data**. With HTML5, we get several new attributes to support the `form` and `input` elements.

Some of these attributes are as follows:

autocomplete	height and width
autofocus	list
form	min and max
formaction	multiple
formenctype	pattern (regexp)
formmethod	placeholder
formnovalidate	required
formtarget	step

There are still some gaps in browser support for these attributes, but with the new IE10, Microsoft has promised to bridge this gap to maximum capacity.

Here are some of the most commonly used attributes for HTML5 form elements:

- Putting in practice, for autofocus:

  ```
  First name: <input type="text" name="fname" autofocus="autofocus">
  ```

- Using an image for a button:

  ```
  <input type="image" src="images/submit.png" alt="Submit">
  ```

- Required field:

  ```
  Email: <input type="text" name="email" required>
  ```

- Placeholder text in a form input:

  ```
  <input type="text" name="fname" placeholder="First name">
  ```

Input types

Furthermore, the new input types in HTML5 reduce a lot of additional scripting required by the developers. These new input types are:

color	range
date	search
datetime	tel
datetime-local	time
email	url
month	week
number	

All the new input types are supported by Google Chrome and Opera at the time this book is being written, but there are still some inconsistencies with other browsers.

Let's have a look at some of the applications of these input types:

- Color picker:
```
Select color: <input type="color" name="color">
```
- Date picker:
```
Date of birth: <input type="date" name="dob">
```
- Validated e-mails:
```
E-mail: <input type="email" name="emailadd">
```
- Range selector:
```
<input type="range" name="points" min="1" max="10">
```

How it works...

HTML5 standardizes common coding practices and creates a set of more semantically-orientated sectioning tags (for example, `header`, `nav`, `footer`, and so on). This promotes machine-readability, interoperability, and reusability of content data.

Eliminating all of the repetitive content in the `DOCTYPE` declaration and primary syntax, which announces the document to the browser and other applications about its format, makes it easier for the developers to structure and organize the content.

With the removal of the need to overuse the `DIV` tags with `ID` or `CLASSES` by the introduction of semantic sectioning tags such as `header`, `footer`, `nav` and so on, the code now looks much cleaner and semantically correct.

There's more...

One might need some clarifications about the utilities of specific tags that can be used in place of each other. The **Section versus Article** and **Menu versus Nav** tags are explained here.

Section versus Article

There are still some arguments about the nesting of the `<section>` and `<article>` tags among the developers' community. Some developers prefer to call the content `DIV` as `<section>` and put multiple `<article>` tags inside, and some prefer to have one `<article>` tag with multiple `<section>` tags.

An `article` tag is recommended to be used for a piece of content that could be syndicated in its entirety and still make sense in a different context (as in a magazine article).

The `section` tag is generally recommended to be used in a page of content to denote an area that is thematically distinct from another area on a page; for example, a news area and a blog area.

Menu versus Nav

Just like `section` and `article`, we have another set of similar sounding elements in `nav` and `menu`.

According to W3C, the `nav` element represents a section of a document that links to other documents or to parts within the document itself; that is, a section of navigation links and the `menu` element is used to define context menus and toolbars.

In short, use `nav` for main navigation and `menu` for on-page applications.

Microformats – the smarter Web (Should know)

According to `www.microformats.org`:

> "*Designed for humans first and machines second, microformats are a set of simple, open data formats built upon existing and widely adopted standards.*"

Though **microformats** already existed and was much in practice prior to the HTML5 specifications announcement from W3C, their common motto of a semantic way of coding enhanced the status of microformats many fold.

Using microformats does not affect any visual aspect of the web page, but these selectors can be used to style the presentation of the data if required.

Getting ready

To begin with, let us have a look at the common microformats in use:

Published microformats

Published microformats were standardized by W3C even before the HTML5 specifications were released. The use of these microformats is heavily recommended and encouraged.

- Compound microformats
    - **hCard**: This defines the contact information for people and organizations
    - **hCalendar**: This defines time-based information, such as events
    - **XOXO**: This defines outlines

- Elemental (simple) microformats:
    - **hAtom**: This is used for marking up Atom feeds from within the standard HTML
    - **adr**: This defines postal addresses
    - **geo**: This defines geographical coordinates (latitude, longitude)
    - **hMedia**: This defines audio/video content
    - **hNews**: This defines news content
    - **hProduct**: This defines data about products
    - **hRecipe**: This defines data about recipes and foodstuffs
    - **hResume**: This defines data such as resumes or CVs
    - **hReview**: This defines reviews
    - **rel-directory**: This is used for distributed directory creation and inclusion
    - **rel-enclosure**: This defines multimedia attachments to web pages
    - **rel-license**: This defines the specification of a copyright license
    - **rel-nofollow**: This performs an attempt to discourage third-party content spam (for example, spam in blogs)
    - **rel-tag**: This is used for decentralized tagging (folksonomy)
    - **xFolk**: This defines tagged links
    - **XHTML Friends Network** (**XFN**): This is used for social relationships
    - **VoteLinks**: This is used to indicate agreement or disagreement with, or indifference to, the link's destination

Draft microformats

There are a few microformats that are under development, which we can choose to implement as and when necessary by keeping the future in sight:

- **hAudio**: This defines audio files and references to released recordings
- **citation**: This defines citing references
- **currency**: This defines amount details of money
- **figure**: This is used to associate captions with images
- **geo extensions**: This defines names of places on Mars, the Moon, and other such bodies. It also stores data about altitudes and collections of waypoints marking routes or boundaries
- **species**: This defines the names of living things (already used by Wikipedia and the BBC Wildlife Finder)
- **measure**: This defines physical quantities and structured data-values

Now, we need to list out all generic properties of content, which can be shared with various devices. Documents and purposes such as dates can be used in calendars, e-mail addresses can be used for address books, a street address can be utilized by a maps application, or a CV can be searched by a simple bot if it was defined with `hResume`.

How to do it...

Let us take an example of the most common usage of microformats.

hCard

Every website generally has a contact page with a registered address of the organization behind it. In general, addresses are formed by some common attributes, such as the organization name, contact person, building number, street name, city, state, postal code, country, phone number, e-mail address, and so on.

For example, the contact details of Packt Publishing, the publishing house for this book is:

Packt Publishing Limited
2nd Floor, Livery Place
35 Livery Street
Birmingham
B3 2PB
T +44 0121 265 6484
F +44 0121 212 1419
`contact@packtpub.com`

To format this address in HTML without microformats should be simple.

```
<p>
Packt Publishing Limited<br />
2nd Floor, Livery Place<br />
35 Livery Street<br />
Birmingham<br />
B3 2PB<br />
T +44 0121 265 6484<br />
F +44 0121 212 1419 <br />
<a href="mailto:contact@packtpub.com">contact@packtpub.com</a><br />
</p>
```

A simple and very common coding practice! But does it mean something to the browser or the crawlers, other than just being another paragraph tag with some links and line breaks? No.

Now, we add the hCard microformat to the previous data:

```
<div class="vcard">
<div class="fn org">Packt Publishing Limited</div>
<div class="adr">
<div class="street-address">2nd Floor, Livery Place, 35 Livery
Street</div>
<div><span class="locality">Birmingham</span>,
   <span class="postal-code">B3 2PB</span></div>
<div class="country-name">UK</div>
</div>
<div>Phone: <span class="tel">+44 0121 265 6484</span></div>
<span class="tel"><span class="type">Fax</span>:
<span class="value">+44 0121 212 1419</span></span>
<div>Email: <span class="email"><a href="mailto:contact@packtpub.
com">contact@packtpub.com</a></span></div>
<div>
<span class="tel"><span class="type">Fax</span>:
<span class="value">+1-415-882-0495</span></span>
</div>
</div>
```

The attributes for hCard microformats are as follows:

vcard	email
fn	bday
org	honorific-prefix
adr	honorific-suffix
street-address	label
locality	logo
postal-code	nickname
country-name	note
tel	photo
fax	post-office-box

Date/Time

With HTML5, the new entrant in microformats is **Date/Time**. By enhancing the new tag <time>, we can define the page's age, content relevancy, and calendar support for various devices.

```
<time>2012-11-05</time>
```

The `time` element from HTML5 gives a time definition to the content which is to follow. Now, let's add some microformats to it:

```
<time datetime="2012-11-05">5<sup>th</sup> November</time>
```

The `datetime` as a single attribute covers both date and time, in one definition. If we have to define just the time and not the date then we can do the following:

```
<time datetime="20:00">starting at 8pm</time>
```

Now, together:

```
<time datetime="2012-11-05T20:00+00:00">5<sup>th</sup> November, 8pm
for the party</time>
```

Dates can be defined just by the year number, year-month, year-Wxx (where xx is the week number of that year), and as we have seen in the preceding example, `-T` for the time declaration following the date. The value `+00:00` can be manipulated with the GMT time difference to define the local time.

The preceding declaration will be satisfactory enough for various browsers and devices to allow the visitor to add a calendar item or a reminder of that event.

rel-nofollow

The `rel-nofollow` microformat has been used by SEO-motivated developers for many years now. `rel-nofollow` as an attribute in any `<a>` tag tells the crawlers that the following link is an external website or contains data, which the website does not require to be crawled or listed in search results.

```
<a href="http://www.example.com" rel="nofollow">Other Website<a>
```

How it works...

Microformats use various class names and attributes to define the properties of the specific type of data following them. This data can be identified by browsers, devices, and crawlers alike. The simple implementation of `hCard` in the web page gives the crawlers a sense of authenticity of the information and organizational behavior.

Similarly, Date/Time can also be implemented with the publishing date of the specific page to make sure that crawlers identify it as the latest information and keep the higher ranking as it is.

There's more...

The application of microformats is critical for the extendibility of data beyond the primary application.

Extended data

In the days of multi-device, multi-platform Internet, the information is not bound to the standard HTML visualization anymore. The smarter the content of a web page is, the more useful it can be for various applications.

Many XML-based applications, crawlers, bots, and algorithms are being developed everyday to identify and sort the content in a meaningful way. While HTML5 is redefining the complete approach to coding, microformats are busy making a new smarter Web.

Play it on – multimedia (Must know)

Since the inception of HTML, one question has often been debated in the developer community. Why do we have an `img` tag for images but there are no `video` or `audio` tags to support video or audio files natively? The answer to this question was another question about the size of audio/visual files and the speed of the Internet.

In recent years, the Internet has transformed. Video-sharing websites such as YouTube and Vimeo made it an everyday practice for visitors to upload, share, and watch multimedia online. This was possible only with third-party software plugins such as Adobe Flash, integrated components from Quicktime Player, Realplayer, or Windows Media Player.

In each of these scenarios, it became essential for the visitor to have these software and supportive plugins installed locally on their computer. Moreover, there was still no standardization about which plugin format should be used by the website visited for video purposes.

Loading of all these extensions and plugins within the browser takes a lot of time, resulting in a very slow responding computer and connection.

With faster Internet connectivity, browser support, and standardized approach definitions from HTML5, native file formats' support for video and audio for browsers has solved this problem. Well, almost.

Getting ready

First up, get that analysis of the website we did earlier in the book to see the ratio of browsers used by the visitors in recent times.

The `<video>` and `<audio>` tags are supported by all the browsers, including IE but only IE9 or higher.

The second move would be to have your media files in `.ogv`, `.mp4`, and `.webm` for video, and `.ogg` and `.mp3` for audio. The various file formats for every file will be left for the browsers to select and play the best format they support.

How to do it...

The `<video>` and `<audio>` elements in HTML5 are not much different from the `<img>` element for an image. The only visible difference would be the full use of the text without abridging to three characters and an independent closing tag.

Video

This is how we embed the video in an HTML5 document:

```
<video src="movie.webm"></video>
```

If the visitor comes from a browser that does not support the `video` tag, we can add a message to inform them about the inconvenience.

```
<video src="movie.webm">
This is fallback content to display if the browser does not support
the video element.
</video>
```

To resolve the individual format support for the browsers, we can provide options to the browser itself:

```
<video>
<source src="movie.webm" />
<source src="movie.ogv" />
<source src="movie.mp4" />
<p>This is fallback content</p>
</video>
```

Now, we add a few best practices such as video controls, placeholder image, type, and codec information for the videos:

```
<video poster="movie.jpg" controls>
<source src="movie.webm" type='video/webm; codecs="vp8.0, vorbis"'/>
<source src="movie.ogv" type='video/ogg; codecs="theora, vorbis"'/>
<source src="movie.mp4" type='video/mp4; codecs="avc1.4D401E,
mp4a.40.2"'/>
<p>This is fallback content</p>
</video>
```

As you can imagine, the `poster="movie.jpg"` declaration refers to an image that will be displayed in the place of the video till the visitor clicks on the controls to play the video.

The `type` and `codecs` attributes are included to tell the browser the specific compression version or format used in that particular file, hence saving the time it will spend on scanning the video and matching the compression from the library of inbuilt codecs.

Audio

Once you have understood the `video` element, the `audio` element follows suit.

```
<audio controls>
<source src="horse.ogg" type="audio/ogg">
<source src="horse.mp3" type="audio/mpeg">
Your browser does not support the audio element.
</audio>
```

The controls can be used just as in the preceding example or as `controls="controls"`, depending upon the developer's method of choice.

How it works...

As mentioned earlier, the arrival of the native `video` and `audio` elements of HTML was delayed because of the speed and data size practicalities on the networks.

In the developed and hotly contested browser market, the browser vendors are still calling the shots when it comes to adaptation of any new browser-based technologies. This is exactly why we need multiple file formats for both the audio and video files on the server. The browsers choose the file format that *they* have proper licensing agreements to support and leave the rest as it is. If nothing suitable is found, the placeholder message appears for the visitor.

There's more...

It is not always practical to have multiple file formats of media files because of their file sizes. The best approach for developers here is to decide on the range of browsers they are planning to support and what format is commonly supported.

File formats

Here is a list of file formats supported by various browsers natively with these two elements:

Video formats			
Browser	**MP4**	**WebM**	**Ogg**
Internet Explorer 9	YES	NO	NO
Firefox 4.0	NO	YES	YES
Google Chrome 6	YES	YES	YES
Apple Safari 5	YES	NO	NO
Opera 10.6	NO	YES	YES

Audio formats			
Browser	**MP3**	**Wav**	**Ogg**
Internet Explorer 9	YES	NO	NO
Firefox 4.0	NO	YES	YES
Google Chrome 6	YES	YES	YES
Apple Safari 5	YES	YES	NO
Opera 10.6	NO	YES	YES

In a general recommendation, `.mp4` and `.ogv` for video, and `.mp3` and `.ogg` for audio covers pretty much all browser platforms.

The mobile – the seamless experience (Become an expert)

For a long period of time, the standard desktop resolution used to be 800 x 600. There were no doubts in the web developers' and designers' minds about the width of the container or wrapper they were choosing.

All the websites had a temporary 760-pixel width defined and hardcoded in the code. When resolutions jumped universally to 1024 x 768, all the web professionals moved to almost 980 pixels in their choice of width for any web page.

So now, when the devices, which are used to browse the website, range from high-resolution tablet computers and smartphones, to your refrigerator (no kidding!), we cannot depend on hardcoded fixed-width coding practices.

Getting ready

Media queries have been around for a long time and is valid even now with surprising friendliness with the browsers.

They were present with previous versions of HTML as well as CSS2. If you can recall the small syntaxes such as the following:

```
<link rel="stylesheet" type="text/css" media="screen" href="style.
css">
<link rel="stylesheet" type="text/css" media="print" href="print.css">
```

The `media="screen"` or `media="print"` declaration made sure that when the page is displayed on a device screen, it uses the `style.css` file, and when it is sent to a printer, the properties in the `print.css` file are inherited by the document.

Now, the `print.css` file may just contain a completely different font face, width, image sizing, or a new layout altogether or we can have just one CSS file with specific CSS properties for a specified media:

```
@media print {
        * { font-family: serif }
}
```

It is not possible for any developer or designer to test their website on each and every device-browser combination available out there. This is where we have to go back on the analysis we did in the beginning of the book. It may look insignificant in numbers, but considering how the website might be rendered on those devices, it may cause the visitors to not return or continue browsing on your website.

How to do it...

The media type element is defined by using `@media` and supports the following media types:

print	screen
aural	tty
braille	tv
handheld	embossed
all	speech
projection	3d-glasses

The most common media types in practice are `screen` and `print`.

The @media rule

For the following examples, we will take *less than* 600px for mobile, a *minimum* of 900px for tablet computers, a combination of both of these sizes in one query for specific media support, and finally for higher screen resolutions.

```
@media screen and (max-width: 600px) { … }
@media screen and (min-width: 900px) { … }
@media screen and (min-width: 600px) and (max-width: 900px) { … }
@media screen and (min-width: 900px) { … }
```

Common styles can be defined outside of the `@media` element regularly.

The HTML call for the styles from media queries is the same, and at no point needs any additional treatment.

```
    @media screen and (max-width: 600px) {
       #wrapper{
width:480px;
```

```
}
}
   @media screen and (min-width: 600px) and (max-width: 900px) {
      #wrapper{
width:600px;
}
}
   @media screen and (min-width: 900px) {
      #wrapper{
width:900px;
}
}
```

Too much confusion too soon? There is another way!

The @import rule

The `@import` rule allows you to send media queries to the browsers and imports the corresponding style rules from an external CSS file:

```
@import url(one.css) (min-width:400px);
@import url(two.css) (min-width:600px);
@import url(three.css) (min-width:800px);
```

These regular files not only save you the trouble of keeping track of the nesting parameters in multiple curly brackets, but also only load the required piece of code if necessary.

Other than the `min-width` and `max-width` parameters, the queries can be set for various different purposes such as:

- Dimensions:

  ```
  @media (min-device-width: 640px) { ... }
  @media (max-device-height: 720px) { ... }
  ```

- Device Aspect Ratio:

  ```
  @media screen and (device-aspect-ratio: 16/9) { ... }
  ```

- Device Orientation:

  ```
  @media screen and (orientation:portrait) { ... }
  ```

- Color:

  ```
  @media screen and (color) { ... }
  @media screen and (monochrome) { ... }
  @media screen and (min-color-index: 256) { ... }
  ```

How it works...

An option-based CSS call from the HTML document loads the stylesheet only once, and does not respond when the orientation changes or when the browser window resizes. It also causes an unnecessary server connection to check and return with a different CSS file based on the device.

With media queries defined in the CSS file, it simplifies the way a web page reacts to the stylesheet. It allows the identifiers to inherit the properties from the stylesheet without causing multiple connections to the server and delays in the loading of the web page.

There's more...

In the fast-paced web market, it always helps when a developer knows the user preferences in hard numbers.

The current trends

If we have a look at the report on global trends in `www.StatusCounter.com`, it is evidently clear that with the rise of 3G and 4G networks worldwide, mobile browsing is definitely on the rise.

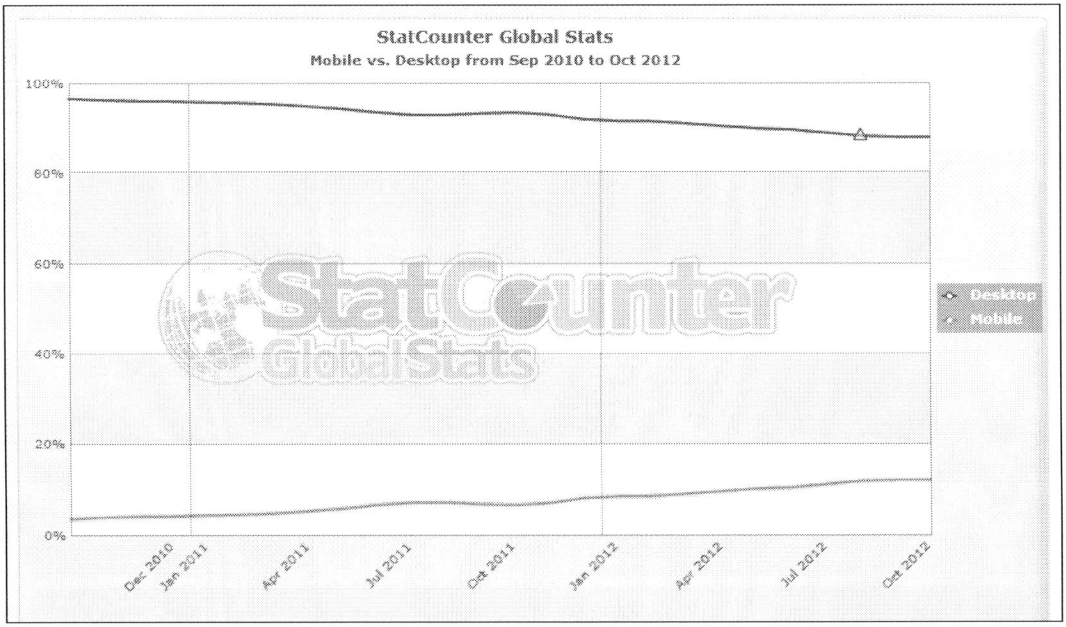

Another statistic for a relatively shorter period of time can provide us with the details of device browsers that were used for mobile browsing for more accurate queries and implementation:

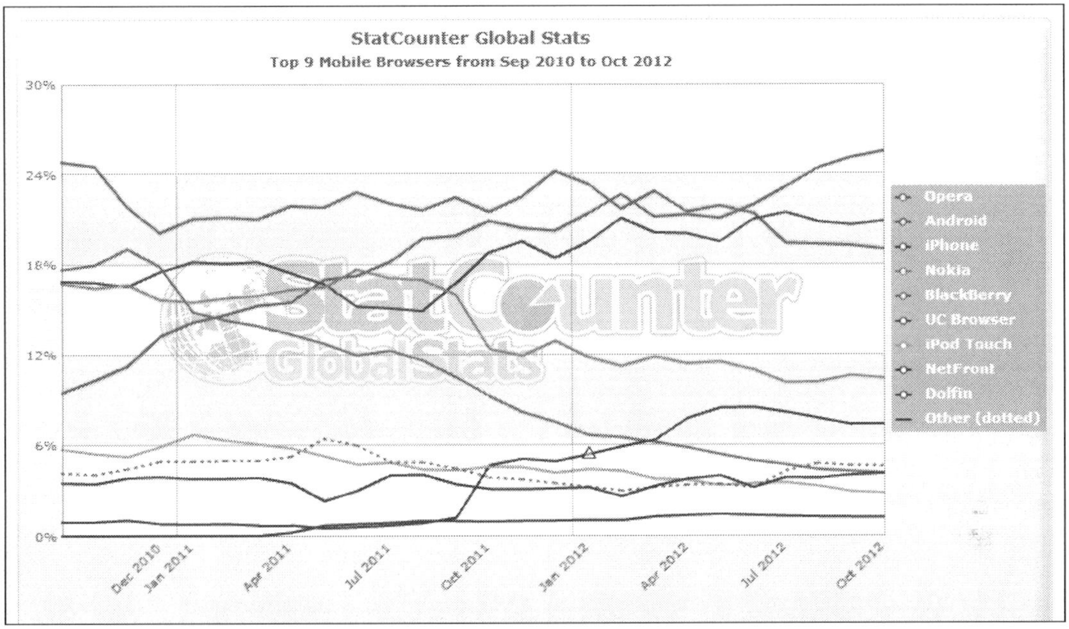

RIA – Canvas (Become an expert)

If you started your career in web design or development in the late 90s to early 2000s, there is definitely a good chance that at some point, you've been asked to do a zany, cool, and bouncy website using (then) Macromedia Flash.

After it was acquired by Adobe in 2005, Flash transformed from being a stage-based, procedural script-running, hard-coded, and embedded object to a **Rich Internet Application** (**RIA**).

With the arrival of Adobe Flex as an SDK for Flash's Action Script 3.0, the company tried to lure more developers into Flash development. Later, Adobe donated Flex to the Apache foundation. All this, and yet no browser vendor ever released the Flash plugin integrated with any of their products.

Flash-based applications took time to develop, never had any open source frameworks supporting the final product, and came across many memory-hogging security threats. The biggest blow to this technology came when Apple decided not to support Flash with any of the iPad, iPhone, or iPod devices.

The message was loud and clear. The web needed a new platform to support Rich Internet Applications, which can be seamlessly integrated in browsers without any third-party plugin requirement at the visitors' end.

Presenting HTML5 Canvas.

Getting ready

The HTML5 `canvas` element provides a canvas (surprise!) with a specified height and width inside a web page, which can be manipulated with JavaScript to generate graphics and Rich Internet Applications.

How to do it...

It is just the same as it was with video or audio.

```
<canvas id="TestCanvas" width="300" height="300">
Your browser does not support Canvas element from HTML5.
</canvas>
```

The preceding syntax gives us a blank block element with the specified height and width, which can now be identified with some JavaScript by the ID `TestCanvas`.

```
<script>
var test=document.getElementById("TestCanvas");
var col1=c.getContext("2d");
col1.fillRect(0,0,20,80);
col1.fillStyle="#808";
</script>
```

A variable named `test` is defined with the method `document.getElementByID()` to identify a canvas on the web page.

The `getContext` object, which is a built-in HTML5 object, is defined in another variable called `col1`. The value `2d` provides properties and methods for drawing paths, boxes, circles, text, images, and more.

The `fillRect(x,y,width,height)` method provides four parameters to draw a rectangle on the x and y coordinates. Similarly, the `fillStyle()` method defines the fill color of the drawing.

The output is as follows:

The origin of the x and y coordinates lies at the top-left corner of the canvas, unlike the graph paper (which most of us are used to), where it lies in the bottom-left corner.

Appending the graph for multiple columns by additional `getContext` variables can be done as follows:

```
<script>
var test=document.getElementById("TestCanvas");
var col1=test.getContext("2d");
col1.fillStyle="#808";
col1.fillRect(10,0,20,80);
var col2=test.getContext("2d");
col2.fillStyle="#808";
col2.fillRect(40,0,20,100);
var col3=test.getContext("2d");
col3.fillStyle="#808";
col3.fillRect(70,0,20,120);
</script>
```

We get the following output:

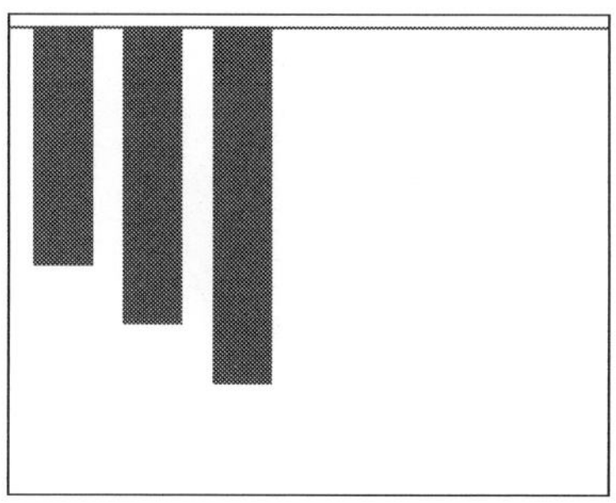

The `getContext` variables can be defined with different methods as well.

To draw a line we use the `moveTo(x,y)` and `lineTo(x,y)` methods:

```
line.moveTo(10,10);
line.lineTo(150,250);
line.stroke();
```

The `moveTo()` method defines the starting point of the line and the `lineTo()` method defines the end point on the x and y coordinates. The `stroke()` method without any value assigned to it connects the two assigned points with a line stroke.

The `stroke()` and `fill()` are the ink methods used to define the visibility of the graphic.

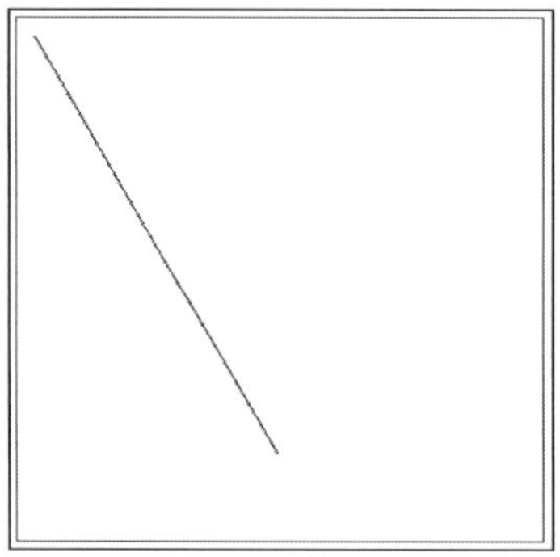

To draw a circle we use the `arc(x,y,r,start,stop)` method:

```
circle.beginPath();
circle.arc(150,150,80,0,2*Math.PI);
circle.fill();
```

With the `arc()` method, we must use either the `fill()` method or the `stroke()` method for a visible area.

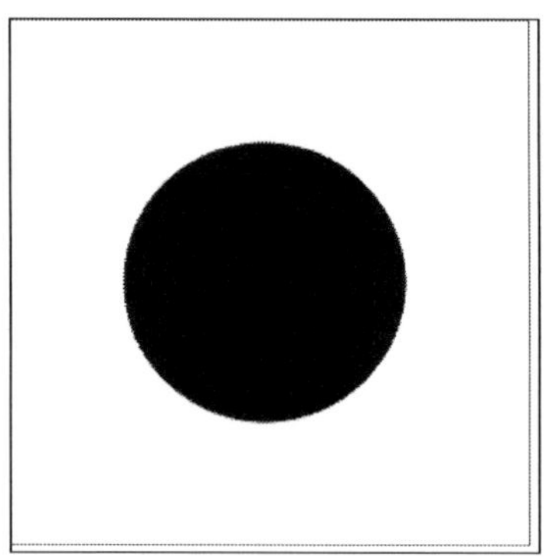

For further exploration, here are a few more canvas methods that can be tried out:

Text for canvas:

- `font`: This specifies font properties for text
- `fillText(text,x,y)`: This draws normal text on the canvas
- `strokeText(text,x,y)`: This draws stroked text without any fill color

Here are the syntaxes for the preceding properties:

```
text.font="30px Arial";
text.fillText("HTML5 Canvas",10,50);
text.strokeText("HTML5 Canvas Text",10,100);
```

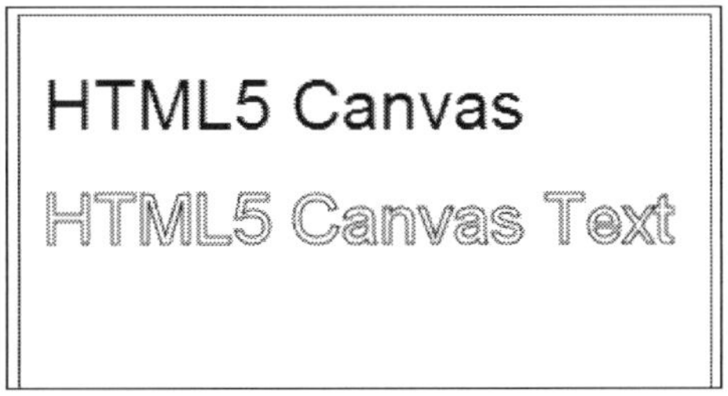

And for the last example, we will do a raster image drawing using the ID into the canvas:

```
var img=document.getElementById("canvas-bg");
draw.drawImage(img,10,10);
```

Similar to the ID for Canvas, the image ID is selected by the `document.getElementById()` method, and then we can use it as a background for the selected canvas.

The image used with the ID `canvas-bg` can be placed in a hidden `div` tag and later can be used as a background for any graph or chart, or any other graphic. One of the most practical applications of the text and image drawing on a canvas could be the customization of a product with label image and text over it.

How it works...

There are many places where Canvas may be implemented for regular web development practices. It can be used to generate real-time charts, product customization applications, or more complex or simple applications, depending on the requirement.

We know that Canvas is an HTML5 element and the key (for Canvas) always remains with the JavaScript used in it. We get support from all the browsers apart from IE8 or below.

There's more...

It always helps when a developer knows about the resources available at their disposal.

Open source JS frameworks for Canvas

There are many open source JavaScript frameworks and libraries available for easy development of the graphics with Canvas. A few noteworthy ones are **KineticJS** and **GoJS**. Another framework is **ThreeJS**, which uses WebGL and allows 3D rendering for your web graphics.

CSS3 – beautiful yet powerful (Should know)

CSS3, with every new specification involved in this release, powers HTML5 in every step of the way. Just as the case was with cutting down code length and fewer server connections in HTML5, CSS3 takes the trend even further.

This is achieved not by any fundamental changes in the existing coding practices, but with the introduction of some of the most commonly used styles as native properties, such as gradients, rounded corners, drop shadows, and external fonts.

For each of the previously mentioned design styles or properties, designers used images, which caused multiple server connections and larger page sizes.

Getting ready

As a designer, it was a routine to use some of the basic design effects to achieve the impact your client or managers have requested. Have a look at your website and list down if the following properties can be seen on the web page:

- **Image-based text**: Used because the font may not be found in the visitors' device
- **Rounded corners for boxes**: Used to highlight a specific bit of information or buttons
- **Drop shadow effect from Photoshop**: Used for the whole page or headings or specific sections of the content, including the navigation
- **Gradient background**: Uses small (often 1px wide) PNG files to tile with CSS
- **Semi-transparent background tiles**: Used for a glossy effect for the whole web page on image backgrounds
- **Backgrounds**: Uses large image files
- **Hover animation effects**: Used for animation using JS or Flash

Now, ready with the list, let us see how we can do it with CSS and without using external images or JavaScript. All the things we are going to try here are supported by all the browsers in general (sometimes with a few hacks) and IE9 and above.

How to do it...

As usual, IE8 or below may not support a few of these properties but the rest are good to go.

External fonts

The advantage of using external fonts is that now, without worrying about web-safe fonts, or in other words, fonts which can be found by default on visitors' computers, designers can be more creative without retreating to image-based text.

There are two methods to integrate external fonts in CSS3.

Local fonts

Locally stored fonts are located on the server just like images or other script files, and are imported in the CSS file on load and later are used as font properties.

```
@font-face {
font-family: 'Marcellus SC';
src: url('fonts/Marcellus.ttf'),
url('fonts/Marcellus.eot'); /*IE9 and above*/
}
```

Once defined, it can be used at various places as defined regularly:

```
h1{
font-family: 'Marcellus SC';
font-size: 1.5em;
}
```

Web fonts

Web fonts are imported from the repositories held at third-party servers. The **Google Webfonts library** is the best known resource for the job and can be accessed at `http://www.google.com/webfonts`.

The fonts can be integrated from external websites in different ways. You can integrate them in the web page by doing the following:

```
<linkhref="http://fonts.googleapis.com/css?family=Marcellus+SC"
rel="stylesheet" type="text/css">
```

You can also import in a CSS file by applying the following code snippet:

```
@import url(http://fonts.googleapis.com/css?family=Marcellus+SC);
```

The call from the CSS file for the fonts remains the same as described in the local fonts section.

Drop shadow

Most managers and clients just love using drop shadows. It gives the design a little elevation and depth, which is needed sometimes.

Most often used for navigation bars or for the whole container, the only way drop shadows were used before now was by using Photoshop-edited graphics.

There are two types of shadow options given in CSS3 specifications.

Box shadow

Box shadow is used for block elements and works for the whole area and not for the specific text inside it.

```
#shadow{
box-shadow:1px 1px 5px #333;
}
```

The four parameters are horizontal shadow, vertical shadow, and the fade or blur distance of the effect, and color of the shadow. Another parameter called `inset` can be used if an inner shadow is required in place of a drop shadow.

When this property is called in as the ID property for a given DIV, here is what we get:

Also notice the use of external fonts from the preceding example.

Text shadow

The other shadow property's utility is clear by its name. Text shadow is used when we need to have a shadow for the text.

```
h1{
    text-shadow:2px 2px 2px #C30;
}
```

This will get us:

The text shadow property is not supported by any version of IE as of IE9.

Rounded corners

Designers spend hours sorting out those four corners for any box design if it involves rounded corners. If they are present in multiple shapes or sizes, or even colors, the image directory often gets filled with these tiny images.

Not any more, says CSS3:

```
border-radius:10px;
-moz-border-radius:10px; /* To support with Firefox 3.6 and earlier */
```

And here is what we get:

A little more adventure:

```
border-bottom-right-radius:25px;
border-top-left-radius:25px;
-moz-border-bottom-right-radius:25px;
-moz-border-top-left-radius:25px;
```

Gradients

The following example is another image-oriented task simplified by CSS3 gradients. And here is how to do it:

```
.gradient-bg {
background-image: -webkit-linear-gradient(top, #2F2727, #1a82f7);
background-image: -moz-linear-gradient(top, #2F2727, #1a82f7);
background-image: -ms-linear-gradient(top, #2F2727, #1a82f7);
background-image: -o-linear-gradient(top, #2F2727, #1a82f7);
}
```

Looks tacky, doesn't it? So allow me to explain how this works.

The `gradient` property from CSS3 is supported by all browsers, but they do it by their own syntax. The general syntax is not supported by any of the browsers and it is definitely hilarious. Here is what W3C has proposed:

```
background-image: linear-gradient(top, #2F2727, #1a82f7);
```

And here are the browser-specific CSS declarations:

```
/* Safari 5.1+, Mobile Safari, Chrome 10+ */
background-image: -webkit-linear-gradient(top, #2F2727, #1a82f7);
/* Firefox 3.6+ */
background-image: -moz-linear-gradient(top, #2F2727, #1a82f7);
/* IE 10+ */
background-image: -ms-linear-gradient(top, #2F2727, #1a82f7);
/* Opera 11.10+ */
background-image: -o-linear-gradient(top, #2F2727, #1a82f7);
}
```

Among the three parameters in the preceding code snippet, the first one tells us the location of the linear gradient to start and the remaining two are the colors. Moreover, the `gradient` property can be controlled by various parameters. These include `radial-gradient`, `left top`, `left bottom` and so on.

Since the `gradient` property is only supported in IE10, definition of the fallback background colors or images, before the gradient property, is advisable.

Opacity

To give one block element, usually a DIV, some translucent background the `opacity` property from CSS3 is used. The common implementation comes for websites, which are designed with an image-based background.

The declaration of the property is quite simple and uses scales from `0` to `1` where `0` means completely transparent and `1` means opaque:

```
div { opacity: 0.5;}
```

Opacity is generally supported by all browsers including IE9 and above. For IE8 and below, the declaration varies as follows with a scale from `0` to `100`:

```
div {opacity: Alpha(opacity=50);}
```

Background sizing

The background sizing property allows us to use an image in the background with scaling properties.

```
body
{
```

```
background: url(background.png);
background-size: 100%;
background-repeat: no-repeat;
}
```

This reduces the image file size used in the background to a considerable size.

Columns

A very helpful property comes in the form of `columns`. This helps to break down the text in a newspaper format in a `DIV` tag.

```
div.threecols
{
columns:100px3;
-webkit-columns:100px 3; /* Safari and Chrome */
-moz-columns:100px 3; /* Firefox */
}
```

This is one of my personal beloved properties in CSS3, but unfortunately doesn't come with any IE support. This should not discourage you from using it, as it will make any visitor from other good browsers pretty pleased with the easy-to-read text.

Transition

Rollover effects from CSS3 come in the form of the transition property.

```
div.transform
{
width:100px;
height:30px;
background:red;
transition:height 2s;
-moz-transition:height 2s; /* Firefox 4 */
-webkit-transition:height 2s; /* Safari and Chrome */
-o-transition:width 2s; /* Opera */
}

div.transform:hover
{
height:50px;
}
```

As it is clear by the two parameters passed in the `transition` property, `height` and `2s` are direction and time in seconds respectively. Transition can be applied with `width` as a parameter of choice.

The hover for the given `DIV` element is defined to trigger the transformation. The call to the given `DIV` is simple:

```
<div class="transform"></div>
```

This is another non-IE property but an excellent one to try out.

There's more...

There are a lot of other new properties in the CSS3 specifications, which are powerful and diverse in their applications.

A few more properties

Here are a few more properties from CSS3 for you to try:

Box-sizing	Font-stretch
Rotation	Word-break
Box-align	Word-wrap
Box-pack	Transform
Content	Nav-index

Data – smart websites (Become an expert)

The most advanced features of HTML5 are about the data. Now, we can develop web-based applications with locally stored files and database on the user's computer. These files can later be accessed without any active Internet connection if there is a data communication between two or more visitors and you do not wish to engage into heavy server traffic.

Offline storage becomes important if we are developing heavy applications for users who are on the move or may not have consistent Internet coverage, and we want to maintain a seamless experience for the visitors.

WebSockets allow visitors to have a communication channel of their own on the web page.

Getting ready

Often, the local storage is used for either mobile-based websites or applications involving big chunks of data. To give the visitor quick access to what they are looking for, it becomes a clever idea to hold the data in a local storage of the computer or mobile device till it is requested.

Google Docs and offline Gmail are two of the many web applications we use on an everyday basis. On the mobile platform, compiled HTML5 apps using tools such as PhoneGap (`http://phonegap.com/`) strongly use local storage.

WebSockets can be found often on the websites of live sports broadcast where visitors can discuss the live events together, or on the tech support websites where the visitors can join in a one-on-one discussion with a representative of the company.

How to do it...

Let's have a look at the local storage first and then WebSockets.

Local storage

Now, we have a website or application, which we want to preload and locally store for the visitor, to be accessed later or while browsing if the Internet connection becomes unstable.

The first thing to remember is the default limit of local storage from HTML5 is 5 MB for mobile devices. If the cached data size exceeds that limit, the visitors will get a message asking them to increase the size of the local storage on their device.

If users accept the notification, the application resumes as intended. Otherwise, the local storage does not cache at all.

The second thing to remember is that all the files or data asked to be cached must be available on the server. The caching takes place on the *everything or nothing* principle.

Appcache

Meet **appcache**, the document type which will tell the browser about all the web pages or resources you wish to store locally. With the extension of `.appcache`, this file holds the manifest of local storage. Here is how you can call the `.appcache` file on the web page:

```
<html lang="en" manifest="offline.appcache">
```

Easy to understand, the syntax is added to the HTML attribute of the web page with an element called `manifest` and here, in a file named `offline.appcache`. The `manifest` must be declared in all the web pages you wish to cache locally.

The .htaccess file

To declare appcache as a new file/MIME type for the server, we need to declare it in the `.htaccess` file *before* trying to cache any data from the server.

Here is what we need to add in the `.htaccess` file on the server:

```
AddType text/cache-manifest .appcache
```

The cache manifest

The valid `.appcache` file can be as small as the primary syntax declaration:

```
CACHE MANIFEST
```

The preceding syntax is essential for every manifest file. Comments in the cache manifest can be declared with a # prefix:

```
# cache manifest for my website v1.0 - Jan-05-2013
```

Every cache manifest has three sections which are listed as follows:

- `CACHE`: This is a list of exact URLs to request and store locally
- `FALLBACK`: These are the files to display when an offline user attempts to access an uncached file
- `NETWORK`: These are the resources that are available only while a user is online

Here is an example of a cache manifest file:

```
CACHE MANIFEST
# cache manifest for my website v1.0 - Jan-05-2013

CACHE:
/css/style.css
/images/logo.png
http://example.com/css/offline.css
http://example.com/index.html
about.html

FALLBACK:
login.html offline-message.html
/ /offline.html
/images /offline.png

NETWORK:
*
```

The `CACHE` is the default property of the cache manifest file. If we are not using the other sections, a simple list of files will make sure that it falls under the `CACHE` section.

The file URLs can be relative or absolute, based on the complexity of the site structure. Any file type, including images, scripts, styles, and HTML documents can be cached in the local storage.

The FALLBACK section defines the default properties if an uncached resource is called. It can be done in different ways as demonstrated in the preceding example, such as direct filename fallback, a common sitewide fallback, or a folder or directory-based fallback for specific file types.

The NETWORK section dictates the list of resources exclusively available when online. The * means that the rest of the website, which is not mentioned in the CACHE section, will need an Internet or network connection.

As mentioned before, everything mentioned in the manifest to be cached, must be available on the server at the time the website is visited with an Internet connection, to be stored locally. It will either cache everything specified in the manifest or nothing at all.

To see the cached files on Chrome, type in `chrome://appcache-internals` in the address bar.

WebSocket

WebSocket is used for two-way communication over a single socket using TCP. Presently, it is still being standardized by the W3C; but, the latest versions of Chrome and Safari have support for WebSocket.

WebSocket is not just a standalone HTML5 feature. In order to use sockets, JavaScript services (generally written with `Node.js`) are used. A basic declaration for a socket is:

```
var Ws = new WebSocket(url, [protocol] );
```

To check if your browser supports sockets, run the following script:

```
<script type="text/javascript">
function WebSocketTest()
{
if ("WebSocket" in window)
  {
alert("WebSocket is supported by your Browser!");
}
else
  {
alert("WebSocket NOT supported by your Browser!");
  }
}
</script>
```

In the event of support availability, we can declare the socket events. The events for a WebSocket include `open`, `close`, `error`, and `message`. The event handlers for each of these events sum up the complete communication between sockets.

Event	Handler	Description
`Open`	`Ws.onopen`	When socket connection is established
`message`	`Ws.onmessage`	When client receives data from server
`error`	`Ws.onerror`	When there is an error in communication
`close`	`Ws.onclose`	When connection is closed

The declaration is based on `Ws`, which is the variable name chosen to declare WebSocket in the example. The WebSocket has two associated methods called `Ws.send()` and `Ws.close()`.

The `send()` method is used to transmit data using the connection. The `close()` method would be used to terminate any existing connection.

Here is a complete example in the previously mentioned context:

```
<script type="text/javascript">
function MyFirstWebSocket()
{
if ("WebSocket" in window)
  {
alert("WebSocket is supported by your Browser! ");
     // Let us open a web socket
var ws = new WebSocket("ws://localhost:9998/echo");
ws.onopen = function()
     {
        // Web Socket is connected, send data using send()
ws.send("Message to send");
alert("Message is sent... ");
     };
ws.onmessage = function (evt)
     {
var received_msg = evt.data;
alert("Message is received... ");
     };
ws.onclose = function()
     {
        // websocket is closed.
```

```
alert("Connection is closed... ");
     };
  }
else
  {
     // The browser doesn't support WebSocket
alert("WebSocket NOT supported by your Browser!");
  }
}
</script>
```

Now call the script in the body:

```
<a href="javascript:MyFirstWebSocket()">Run WebSocket</a>
```

How it works...

WebSockets work on server-based configurations, which work on TCP and can be configured on your localhost WAMP or XAMPP or Apache web servers. Once initiated, the protocol hands over the control to the browser for a specific session time, which allows the visitors to establish a data connection.

The local storage copies all the files mentioned in the `.appcache` file until it is updated. A minor edit in a comment is enough to trigger a fresh reload of the data cached on the browser.

There's more...

Imagination always plays a big role in the adaptation of a new technology. There is a lot of support and there are many creative developers willing to show off what they can do with this new powerful technology!

Sockets in action

There are several examples of WebSockets that can be seen around the Internet, but due to lack of proper browser support, it is still in its teething stages. The best WebSocket chat example can be seen at `http://html5demos.com/web-socket`.

The transferrable Web (Must know)

We tried to keep the focus of topics in this book on how you can migrate the code of the website, without changing any visual appearance, from previous versions of HTML or XHTML to HTML5.

Looking closely, the principal structure for a given web page in HTML5 is similar to others in terms of the primary elements. Web pages can be maintained with a better consistency and quality by developers who did not write them originally.

Results

Now we know that using common element names such as header, footer, section, and article makes it easier for machines to render the relevant information when needed. This makes communication and readability of the code a lot easier.

It becomes easier to document the properties of semantically correct elements in a longer practice and later to maintain them.

Gradient, rounded corners, and drop shadows can be generated in the browsers, without going back to the server and asking it for image files to display.

External fonts allow the designers to consider using text for big graphics-based text, reducing further file size and network time for the browsers.

Local storage and web sockets allows for offline browsing and a peer-to-peer communication channel without putting any real load on to the server.

All this and more is possible because you as a developer or designer wanted it to be.
The faster we adopt HTML5, the better the Internet and the browsers will be.

Future scalabilities

HTML5 specifications are still being written. The delay in the official announcement of completion has led the two responsible groups, **Web Hypertext Application Technology Working Group** (**WHATWG**) and W3C to define the specifications in two separate versions.

W3C's **Snapshot** and WHATWG's **Living Standard** will be two separate HTML5 versions available for the developers. On the one hand, Snapshot will be more defined and bound by rules as a benchmark, while Living Standard from WHATWG on the other hand, will follow the approach of fixing bugs and adding features as we find or develop them.

In simpler terms, WHATWG has decided that there will be no HTML6 and the entirety of HTML5 will be referred to as just HTML in due course.

New tags and adaptation of features will be left to the developer community and browser vendors. It is expected that the ongoing updates will keep the vendors on the edge and will ensure a healthy competition.

There's more...

A few more tags

Here are a few new tags from HTML5, which you might like to explore in due course. Compatibility issues aside, these new tags are good enough to make your imagination fly.

- `<progress>`: This represents the progress of a task
- `<meter>`: This defines a scalar measurement within a known range (a gauge)
- `<command>`: This defines a command button that a user can invoke
- `<mark>`: This defines marked/highlighted text
- `<wbr>`: This defines a possible line break
- `<bdi>`: This isolates a part of text that might be formatted in a different direction
- `<details>`: This defines additional details that the user can view or hide
- `<summary>`: This defines a visible heading for a `<details>` element
- `<keygen>`: This defines a key-pair generator field (for forms)
- `<datalist>`: This specifies a list of predefined options for input controls
- `<output>`: This defines the result of a calculation

In addition to the other new elements, some of the obsolete elements are removed from the HTML5 specifications; they are as follows:

<acronym>	<applet>	<basefont>
<big>	<center>	<dir>
<font>	<frame>	<frameset>
<noframes>	<strike>	<tt>

Cool stuff to try

A wide variety of frameworks and standard scripts are launched by many open source communities based on HTML5. PhoneGap, for one, allows developers to input an HTML5-CSS3-JS website and converts it into a mobile app.

The mobile specific version of jQuery named **jQuery Mobile** is completely in sync with HTML5 and CSS3, which gives it a semantic approach for the core framework.

Many interactive web-based games and Adobe Flash's HTML5 export plugins prove that the future for the `canvas` tag is bright.

All the browser vendors, in order to show off the capabilities of their representative products, have developed HTML5 galleries. These galleries (`http://www.chromeexperiments.com/` for Google Chrome and `https://developer.mozilla.org/en-US/demos/tag/tech:html5` for Firefox) provide an excellent guide in measuring the true caliber and stretched limits of HTML5.

So just get on and move to the next best thing on the websphere. *Move* to HTML5.

[PACKT] PUBLISHING

Thank you for buying

Instant Migration to HTML5 and CSS3 How-to

About Packt Publishing

Packt, pronounced 'packed', published its first book "*Mastering phpMyAdmin for Effective MySQL Management*" in April 2004 and subsequently continued to specialize in publishing highly focused books on specific technologies and solutions.

Our books and publications share the experiences of your fellow IT professionals in adapting and customizing today's systems, applications, and frameworks. Our solution based books give you the knowledge and power to customize the software and technologies you're using to get the job done. Packt books are more specific and less general than the IT books you have seen in the past. Our unique business model allows us to bring you more focused information, giving you more of what you need to know, and less of what you don't.

Packt is a modern, yet unique publishing company, which focuses on producing quality, cutting-edge books for communities of developers, administrators, and newbies alike. For more information, please visit our website: `www.packtpub.com`.

Writing for Packt

We welcome all inquiries from people who are interested in authoring. Book proposals should be sent to `author@packtpub.com`. If your book idea is still at an early stage and you would like to discuss it first before writing a formal book proposal, contact us; one of our commissioning editors will get in touch with you.

We're not just looking for published authors; if you have strong technical skills but no writing experience, our experienced editors can help you develop a writing career, or simply get some additional reward for your expertise.

1982449R00036

Printed in Germany
by Amazon Distribution
GmbH, Leipzig